Reference Manual
for
Writing Rehabilitation Therapy Treatment Plans

Penny Hogberg C.T.R.S.
Mary Johnson C.T.R.S.

Reference Manual

• Penny Hogberg C.T.R.S. • Mary Johnson C.T.R.S. •

for Writing Rehabilitation Therapy Treatment Plans

Venture Publishing, Inc., 1999 Cato Avenue, State College, PA 16801

Production: Richard Yocum
Cover Design: Naomi Q. Gallagher
Manuscript Editing: Michele L. Barbin

Library of Congress Catalogue Card Number 94-61216
ISBN 0-910251-67-3

Table of Contents

This resource manual, developed to aid therapists in writing individual specific treatment goals, is divided into five major domains: Social, Emotional, Intellectual, Physical, and Leisure. Under each domain is a list of goals that contains the required components to be measured in each section. When developing these goals, the following steps must be taken:

(1) Identify the problem that needs to be changed—TARGET SYMPTOM

(2) Determine what outcome is desired—LONG-TERM GOAL

(3) Develop small steps towards achieving the long-term goal—SHORT-TERM GOALS

(4) Identify the action the therapist will take to help the client achieve the short-term goal—INTERVENTION

    The samples provided in this manual are designed to be used as guides to address a variety of target/problem behaviors. The intent is to provide examples of measurable, observable, and obtainable goals from which therapists can create individualized goals for the specific needs of each patient. On the following pages are some examples of how these goals may be modified by changing the percentages, modalities, therapist interventions, etcetera. Hopefully, therapists will not only use these ready-made goals and their revised goals, but will personally develop their own and keep record of them on the blank forms inserted after each page.

Introduction

TARGET SYMPTOM	LONG-TERM GOAL	SHORT-TERM GOAL	INTERVENTION
Unaware of leisure resources.	Patient to be aware of leisure resources.	Patient will be able to identify a minimum of 10 leisure resources available to the public when asked by therapist 75% of the time.	Therapist to educate patient about the availability of leisure resources in the community.

If the patient is ready for discharge to an unfamiliar community area, the short-term goal may be revised to:

		SHORT-TERM GOAL	INTERVENTION
		Patient will be able to identify a minimum of 10 leisure resources available within walking distance of community placement when asked by therapist by (date).	Therapist to educate patient about available resources within walking distance of community placement.

If the patient is expecting to live in a facility for an extended period and is not utilizing available resources, the short-term goal could be revised to:

		SHORT-TERM GOAL	INTERVENTION
		Patient will be able to identify a minimum of 5 leisure resources available within facility and 5 resources available in surrounding community when asked by therapist 50% of the time.	Therapist to educate client about in-house and community leisure resources.

Example — Leisure

Flexibility

TARGET SYMPTOM	LONG-TERM GOAL	SHORT-TERM GOAL	INTERVENTION
Fearful of leaving treatment center.	Patient to be comfortable leaving treatment center.	Patient will attend off-grounds outings a minimum of 2 times monthly.	Therapist to personally invite patient to off-grounds outings.

If the patient is comfortable leaving the treatment center only when accompanied by staff, the goal might be revised to:

		SHORT-TERM GOAL	INTERVENTION
		Patient will participate in 1 off-grounds outing with peer 1 time weekly for 4 consecutive weeks.	Therapist to pair up patients into "buddy system" for off-grounds outings.

If the patient is very uncomfortable leaving grounds and has never attended an off-grounds outing the goal might be revised to:

		SHORT-TERM GOAL	INTERVENTION
		Patient will attend 1 off-ground outing, escorted by staff 1 time monthly.	Therapist to escort patient— reassure patient as needed.

Example—Emotional

Interpersonal

TARGET SYMPTOM	LONG-TERM GOAL	SHORT-TERM GOAL	INTERVENTION
Continually talks about peers/staff in negative manner.	Generally speak about peers/staff in a positive manner.	Patient will need no more than 2 reminders from staff to talk about peers and staff in a positive manner 50% of groups attended.	Therapist to confront patient when speaking negatively in group setting.

If patient is unable to talk in positive manner in group setting at all, the short-term goal could be revised to this:

		Patient will need no more than 3 reminders from staff to talk about peers and staff in a positive manner 1 of 5 groups weekly.	Therapist to confront patient when speaking negatively in group setting and praise patient when speaking in a positive manner.

If the patient only occasionally needs reminders to speak positively about peers, the short-term goal could be revised to this:

		Patient will independently talk about peers in a positive manner 100% of group time 5 of 5 days by (date).	Therapist to praise client in group when speaking positively—confront as necessary.

Example—Social

INTERACTION

- Avoids all opportunity to interact
- Does not respond to questions/comments
- Responds minimally to others
- Lack of eye contact during conversations
- Needs extra prompts to respond to questions/comments
- Slow to respond to questions/comments
- Responds inappropriately to questions comments
- Does not initiate conversation
- Guarded in group situations
- Continually interrupts others during conversations
- Dominates conversation
- Initiates conversation in negative manner
- Continuous intrusive staring
- Frequent swearing in conversations
- Speaks of private matters in a public way
- Exhibits private behavior in public areas
- Inability to stay on topic of conversation

INTERPERSONAL

- Difficulty getting along with peers
- Talks down to peers
- Continually talks about peers/staff in negative manner
- Finds fault in everyone/everything
- Uses friendships for personal gain
- Gains attention through inappropriate sexual actions/remarks
- Does not respect personal boundaries
- Unable to share group materials
- Manipulates conversation to seek compliments
- Manipulates conversation to seek sympathy
- Grandiose conversations

PASSIVE-AGGRESSIVE

- Allows people to infringe on personal rights to gain friendship
- Unable to disagree with anyone
- Unable to say "no" to others
- Relinquished materials to avoid task
- Difficulty accepting compliments
- Unable to compliment others
- Imposes own standards on others
- Compliments others as a manipulative tool
- Antagonizing behavior, e.g., name calling
- Unable to take no for an answer
- Continually panhandles, e.g., cigarettes, money, tangibles

PATIENT-STAFF RELATIONSHIP

- Avoids staff contact
- Unable to take direction from male/female leader
- Challenges group leader's authority
- Unable to show respect to staff—places self on pedestal
- Places staff on pedestal—adversely affecting relations
- Continually seeks staff approval/reassurance
- Seeks staff interaction—avoids peer interaction

Social

TARGET SYMPTOM	LONG-TERM GOAL	SHORT-TERM GOAL	INTERVENTION

Social

Interaction

TARGET SYMPTOM	LONG-TERM GOAL	SHORT-TERM GOAL	INTERVENTION
Avoids all opportunity to interact.	Patient will seek out opportunity for interaction with peers.	Patient will walk to and sit in dayroom with others a minimum of 30 minutes daily.	Therapist will seek out patient and escort to dayroom a minimum of 2 times daily.
		Patient will report to and sit within group perimeter 90% of group time 2 of 5 days.	Therapist will seat patient within group perimeter.
Does not respond to questions/comments.	To respond to questions/comments.	Patient will respond to greeting from therapist 60% of the time.	Therapist to greet patient every encounter.
		Patient will verbally respond to question/comment 1 time per group.	Therapist will give patient the opportunity to respond to questions/comments.
Responds minimally to others.	Increase frequency/duration of response.	Patient will respond to questions with a more than 1 word answer 3 of 5 times during group.	Therapist will ask patient open-ended questions, eliciting more than a one-word answer.
		Patient will have conversation with peer a minimum of 2 minutes in length 3 of 5 groups as observed by therapist by (date).	Therapist will include patient in conversation with peer—encourage socialization.
Lack of eye contact during conversation.	Maintain eye contact during conversation.	Patient will maintain eye contact with therapist during greeting 50% of the time.	Therapist will request patient have eye contact during greeting.
		Patient will maintain eye contact with therapist during conversation 75% of the time.	Therapist will respond to patient only when eye contact is intermittently established.
Needs extra prompts to respond to question/comments.	Will respond to questions without prompts.	Patient will respond to 80% of questions with a maximum of 2 prompts from therapist.	Therapist will prompt patient for reply as necessary.
		Patient will respond to questions without it being repeated 4 of 5 times as observed by therapist.	Therapist will encourage active listening, minimizing the need for repeating.

Social

TARGET SYMPTOM	LONG-TERM GOAL	SHORT-TERM GOAL	INTERVENTION

S o c i a l

Interaction

TARGET SYMPTOM	LONG-TERM GOAL	SHORT-TERM GOAL	INTERVENTION
Slow to respond to questions/comments.	Respond without hesitation to questions/comments.	Patient will respond to questions/comments within 5 seconds of initiations 80% of the time as observed by therapist.	Therapist will encourage and praise immediate responses to questions/comments.
		Patient will respond to questions/comments 80% of the time without hesitation as observed by therapist.	Therapist will provide 1-to-1 opportunities for conversation.
Responds inappropriately to questions/comments.	Patient will respond appropriately to questions/comments.	Patient will respond politely to greeting from therapist 50% of the time.	Therapist to greet patient every encounter.
		Patient will remain on topic when in conversation 50% of the time as observed by therapist.	Therapist will redirect patient to topic of conversation as necessary.
Does not initiate conversations.	Patient will initiate conversations.	Patient will initiate 1 conversation 1 time per group.	Therapist to facilitate opportunities for group input and interaction.
		Patient will initiate conversation with peer 3 times weekly outside of group setting as observed by therapist.	Therapist will remind patient of goal and inquire about progress.
Guarded in group situations.	Patient will express self in group situations.	Patient will disclose 1 fact about self during group discussion a minimum of 1 time weekly.	Therapist will remind patient of goal and praise success.
		Patient will express 1 opinion/thought each group 50% of the time.	Staff to ask for opinion/thoughts a minimum of 1 time per group.

Social

5

TARGET SYMPTOM	LONG-TERM GOAL	SHORT-TERM GOAL	INTERVENTION

S o c i a l

Interaction

TARGET SYMPTOM	LONG-TERM GOAL	SHORT-TERM GOAL	INTERVENTION
Continually interrupts others during conversation.	To interact in turn during conversation.	Patient will speak only when called upon by therapist 50% of the time every group session.	Therapist will periodically call upon patient for comment during group.
		Patient will talk only when doing so does not interrupt others 80% of the time each group session.	Therapist will remind patient to speak in turn when patient interrupts.
Dominates conversation.	Patient will allow active speaker proportionate amount of time for speaking.	Patient will speak for a maximum of 3 minutes each speaking turn.	Therapist to time conversations and interrupt as necessary.
		During a role play situation, patient will be able to identify when a conversation is being dominated 3 of 4 times.	Therapist to provide opportunity for role playing a minimum of 2 times weekly.
Initiates conversation in negative manner.	Initiate conversations in a positive manner.	Patient will practice politely initiating conversation 2 times daily with observation by therapist.	Therapist to clarify expectations and provide practice opportunities.
		Four of 5 initiated conversations by patient in group will be of a positive manner.	Therapist to confront patient when negatively initiating conversation, suggest appropriate approach.
Continuous intrusive staring.	Display appropriate gaze during conversation.	Patient will advert gaze when reminded by therapist 80% of the time while in group setting.	Therapist will confront patient when staring in group.
		Patient will avert gaze from individual when on unit 80% of the time as observed by therapist.	Therapist will remind patient of goal when found staring.

Social

TARGET SYMPTOM	LONG-TERM GOAL	SHORT-TERM GOAL	INTERVENTION

S o c i a l

Interaction

TARGET SYMPTOM	LONG-TERM GOAL	SHORT-TERM GOAL	INTERVENTION
Frequent swearing in conversation.	Swearing kept to a minimum.	Patient will be free from abusive language 100% of group time 3 of 5 groups.	Therapist to confront/discourage swearing in group.
		Patient will be able to demonstrate 2 alternative ways of expressing self without swearing when involved in group discussions 1 time weekly.	Therapist to facilitate group discussion, provide opportunity to express self positively.
Speaks of private matters in public way.	Will speak of private matters in a private way.	Patient will speak quietly when discussing private matters 3 of 4 times as observed by therapist.	Therapist to remind patient to use quiet tone of voice when speaking of private matters.
		Patient will discuss private matters with designated personnel 100% of time as observed by therapist.	Therapist to direct patient to appropriate personnel regarding private matter.
Exhibits private behavior in public areas.	Will not exhibit private behavior in public.	Patient will ask if particular behavior is offensive/inappropriate before exhibiting behavior 100% of group time.	Therapist will confront patient when exhibiting inappropriate/ offensive behaviors.
		Patient will ask to be excused from group to exhibit "behavior" (e.g., scratch self) in private 100% of the time.	Therapist will praise efforts.
Inability to stay on topic of conversation.	Patient will stay on topic of conversation.	Patient will make 1 comment on topic of conversation each group as observed by therapist.	Therapist will redirect patient when patient begins talking off topic.
		Patient will talk only on topic of conversation in group 50% of the time.	Therapist will excuse patient from group if unable to stay on topic after second warning.

Social

TARGET SYMPTOM	LONG-TERM GOAL	SHORT-TERM GOAL	INTERVENTION

S o c i a l

Interpersonal

TARGET SYMPTOM	LONG-TERM GOAL	SHORT-TERM GOAL	INTERVENTION
Difficulty getting along with peers.	Will have positive peer relationships.	Patient will interact positively with peers 10 minutes daily outside of structured group setting as observed by therapist.	Therapist to introduce and facilitate conversation with select peer.
		Patient will engage in 1 leisure activity from leisure contract with peers outside of group time 1 time weekly as observed by therapist.	Therapist request to see leisure contract weekly and encourage follow through.
Talks down to peers.	Patient treats peers as equals.	Patient will verbally acknowledge positives about peers when asked to do so in group by therapist 80% of the time.	Therapist will allow time each group for peers to acknowledge positives in group members.
		Patient will verbally seek/accept peers' opinions 1 time weekly during group task.	Therapist to provide tasks requiring group cooperation.
Continually talks about peers/ staff in a negative manner.	Generally speaks about peers/ staff in a positive manner.	Patient will need no more than 2 reminders from staff to talk about peers/staff in positive manner 50% of groups attended.	Therapist to confront patient when speaking negatively in group setting.
		Patient will make 1 positive statement to peers without staff encouragement 1 time per group.	Therapist to praise positive efforts.

Social

TARGET SYMPTOM	LONG-TERM GOAL	SHORT-TERM GOAL	INTERVENTION

S o c i a l

Interpersonal

TARGET SYMPTOM	LONG-TERM GOAL	SHORT-TERM GOAL	INTERVENTION
Finds fault in everyone/everything.	Able to see positives in people/situations.	Patient will make 1 positive statement about anyone/anything 1 time per group.	Therapist to encourage positive statements throughout group.
		Patient will find and verbalize 1 positive aspect about an otherwise negative situation in group 1 time by (date).	Therapist to give negative scenario and ask patient to find positives within.
Uses friendships for personal gain.	Will be sincere when developing friendships for intrinsic value.	Patient will be able to state 1 instance in group per week of something favorable they did for another for its intrinsic value.	Therapist to remind patient not to seek material goods in exchange for friendships.
		Patient will perform 1 favor without asking for anything in return by (date) group time.	Therapist to demonstrate skill using role playing group.
Gains attention through inappropriate sexual actions/remarks.	Gain attention through socially acceptable means.	Patient will gain therapist attention by calling his name 3 of 5 times.	Remind patient of goal—praise efforts.
		Patient will verbalize 4 socially acceptable ways of getting attention in group by (date).	Therapist to ask for alternative ways to get attention in a group.
Does not respect personal boundaries.	Patient will respect personal boundaries.	Patient will maintain a minimum distance of 2 feet when engaged in 1-on-1 conversation in unit 1 time daily as observed by therapist.	Therapist will explain personal boundary issues and encourage compliance.
		Patient will be able to identify their personal boundary space 100% of the time as requested by therapist.	Therapist will periodically ask patient to identify their personal boundary space—review as necessary.

Social

TARGET SYMPTOM	LONG-TERM GOAL	SHORT-TERM GOAL	INTERVENTION

S o c i a l

Interpersonal

TARGET SYMPTOM	LONG-TERM GOAL	SHORT-TERM GOAL	INTERVENTION
Unable to share group materials.	Patient will be able to share group materials.	Patient will ask for needed materials from peers 70% of the time in groups.	Therapist to remind patient to request rather than grab for materials.
		Patient will independently share needed materials with peers a minimum of 2 times per group.	Therapist to clarify expectation of sharing to patient prior to each group.
Manipulates conversation to seek compliments.	Will engage in conversation only for intrinsic value.	Patient will praise self a minimum of 1 time per conversation in group setting.	Therapist to confront patient when manipulating conversation to seek compliments.
		Patient will ask questions for therapist only when doing so does not mandate a personal compliment 80% of the time when in conversation.	Therapist will request patient to answer own compliment seeking questions.
Manipulates conversations to seek sympathy.	Patient will engage in conversations only for intrinsic value.	Patient will talk about personal problems a maximum of 1 time per group session.	Therapist to redirect when patient begins talking of personal problems/somatic complaints.
		Patient will verbalize 1 positive statement regarding each personal problem mentioned in group 100% the of time.	Therapist will encourage the patient to find the positives in each of their negatives.
Grandiose conversations.	Patient will talk only about realistic facts.	Patient will talk only about realistic facts 75% of group the time.	Therapist will interrupt patient when he or she becomes grandiose in conversation—redirect.
		Patient will be able to identify the grandiose portion of conversation when requested by therapist 75% of the time.	Therapist will request patient to differentiate between realistic and grandiose contents of conversation.

Social

TARGET SYMPTOM	LONG-TERM GOAL	SHORT-TERM GOAL	INTERVENTION

S o c i a l

Passive/Aggressive

TARGET SYMPTOM	LONG-TERM GOAL	SHORT-TERM GOAL	INTERVENTION
Allows people to infringe on personal rights to gain his or her friendship.	Assert rights in peer relationships.	Patient will make assertive statement to peer about personal preference 2 of 3 groups attended.	Therapist to allow patient opportunity to role play assertive behavior.
		Patient will be able to identify when rights have been violated by peers when asked by therapist 50% of the time.	Therapist will intervene when patient's rights are being violated and ask patient to identify violation and give alternative assertive behavior.
Unable to disagree with anyone.	Patient to express personal views.	Patient will role play opposite view of peer 2 times weekly in group.	Therapist to allow opportunity to role play—praise assertive efforts.
		Patient will make 1 assertive/challenging statement to peer 1 time per group 50% of groups attended.	Therapist to facilitate non-threatening group milieu—remind patient of goal prior to each group.
Unable to say "no" to others.	Patient will assertively refuse unwanted request.	Patient will say "no" to request for personal possessions 1 time daily as observed by therapist.	Therapist to praise/encourage assertive behavior.
		Patient will be able to role play an assertive response to unwanted request 1 time weekly in group.	Therapist to demonstrate assertive response, allow opportunity to role play.
Relinquishes materials to avoid task.	Patient to retain materials needed to complete task.	Patient to relinquish only un-needed materials to peers in group 80% of the time.	Therapist to remind patient to keep needed items.
		Patient to request and keep needed materials to complete task when in group 100% of the time.	Therapist to structure group requiring patients to request materials in order to complete task.

Social

TARGET SYMPTOM	LONG-TERM GOAL	SHORT-TERM GOAL	INTERVENTION

S o c i a l

Passive/Aggressive

TARGET SYMPTOM	LONG-TERM GOAL	SHORT-TERM GOAL	INTERVENTION
Difficulty accepting compliments.	Patient will acknowledge compliments.	Patient will respond "thank you" to 50% of compliments given by therapist by (date).	Therapist to give a minimum of 2 compliments daily to patient.
		Patient will respond "thank you" to praise given by peers in group setting 75% of the time.	Therapist to encourage patient to see and verbalize positives in each other.
Unable to compliment others.	Patient will compliment others.	Patient will verbalize one positive to peer in group when requested by therapist 75% of the time.	Therapist to request patient to verbalize positives a minimum of 1 time per group.
		Patient will initiate compliment to peer(s) a minimum of 2 times weekly during group as observed by therapist.	Therapist to point out positives in others and encourage patient to do so.
Imposes own standards on others.	Allows others to have own standards.	Patient will allow peers to voice own views/standards without trying to persuade to own viewpoint 3 of 5 groups attended.	Therapist to interrupt patient when he or she begins to impose own standards on others.
		Patient will express own views without putting down views of others 50% of the time.	Therapist will facilitate opportunities for patients to express views.
Compliments others as a manipulative tool.	Makes only sincere compliments to others.	Patient will compliment others only when not requesting a favor in return 100% of the time as observed by therapist.	Therapist to confront patient when using compliments to gain favors.
		In role play situations, patient will be able to distinguish between insincere and sincere compliments 3 of 4 times.	Therapist to provide role play situations weekly.

Social

19

TARGET SYMPTOM	LONG-TERM GOAL	SHORT-TERM GOAL	INTERVENTION

S o c i a l

Passive/Aggressive

TARGET SYMPTOM	LONG-TERM GOAL	SHORT-TERM GOAL	INTERVENTION
Antagonizing behavior, e.g., name calling.	Patient will interact with others in a respectful and polite manner.	Patient will be able to identify one example of displayed antagonistic behavior in group as requested by therapist 100% of the time.	Therapist to stop group discussion p.r.n. to discuss displayed antagonistic behavior.
		Patient will verbalize one positive alternative behavior for each displayed antagonistic behavior 50% of the time.	Therapist to brainstorm with patient to discover positive alternative behaviors.
Unable to take "no" for answer.	Patient to be able to accept "no" for an answer.	Patient will correctly answer his or her own previously answered questions when requested by therapist 3 of 4 times in group setting.	Therapist will request patient to answer own repeated question.
		Patient will ask only questions which have not previously been answered by therapist in group setting 3 of 5 times.	Therapist will not respond to previously answered questions—clarify expectations.
Continually panhandles; e.g., cigarettes, money, tangibles.	Patient to rely on self for tangibles.	Patient will supply money and cigarettes to self on 4 of 5 settings.	Therapist to request to see patient's cigarettes/money prior to outing.
		Patient will be able to identify 3 reasons why panhandling is not socially acceptable when requested by therapist 90% of the time.	Therapist to contact patient when panhandling—discuss negatives of panhandling.

Social

TARGET SYMPTOM	LONG-TERM GOAL	SHORT-TERM GOAL	INTERVENTION

S o c i a l

Patient-Staff Relationship

TARGET SYMPTOM	LONG-TERM GOAL	SHORT-TERM GOAL	INTERVENTION
Avoids staff contact.	Patient to have regular staff contact.	Patient to converse with staff/ be in staff proximity a minimum of 1 hour daily as observed by staff.	Therapist to praise patient when conversing with staff/in staff contact.
		Patient will converse with/seek out staff a minimum of 2 times daily in group/on unit.	Therapist to make staff available to patient daily—praise all contact.
Unable to take direction from male/female leader.	Will accept direction from male/ female leader.	Patient will follow leader's direction without complaint 75% of the time in group setting.	Therapist to give concise/firm directions to peers.
		Patient will seek out therapist for direction 1 time daily on unit/in group.	Therapist to make self available to give direction(s) as needed.
Challenges group leader's authority.	Will accept group leader's authority.	Patient will follow 75% of the therapist's instructions question during group time.	Therapist to give clear, concise instructions—encourage compliance.
		Patient will work cooperatively with group leader to complete task 75% of the time during group.	Therapist to provide opportunity to work cooperatively every group.
Unable to show respect to staff—places self on pedestal.	Patient will show respect for staff.	Patient will follow instructions/ advice from staff person 75% of the time offered during group and on the unit.	Staff to offer advice/instructions in a nonauthoritative manner.
		Patient will seek out instructions/ advice from staff person 1 time weekly without prompts either in group or on the unit.	Therapist to make self available for advice/clarification of instructions daily.

Social

TARGET SYMPTOM	LONG-TERM GOAL	SHORT-TERM GOAL	INTERVENTION

S o c i a l

Patient-Staff Relationship

TARGET SYMPTOM	LONG-TERM GOAL	SHORT-TERM GOAL	INTERVENTION
Places staff on pedestal—adversely affecting relationship.	Patient will demonstrate self-respect.	Patient will make one assertive statement regarding patient/staff equality as requested by therapist 1 time every group.	Staff to request assertive statement every group.
		Patient will teach staff/peers rules to 1 leisure activity 1 time when in leisure skills group.	Therapist to request patient to teach skills—encourage efforts.
Continually seeks staff approval/reassurance.	Patient will have sufficient self confidence to complete task alone.	Patient will complete task, asking for advice/reassurance a maximum of 3 times every group.	Therapist to praise abilities prior to starting task.
		Patient will make 3 decisions/choices each group without seeking staff's approval.	Staff to remind patient of goal—encourage compliance.
Seeks staff interaction—avoids peer interaction.	Patient to seek out peer interaction.	When in group, patient will spend 80% of the time interacting with peers 2 of 5 groups.	Therapist to encourage patient-peer interaction.
		Patient to choose peer companionship during 4 of 5 off-grounds outings.	Therapist to encourage peer companionship.

Social

GROUP PERFORMANCE

- Uninvolved in therapies
- Fearful of failing in group situations
- Frustration hinders participation
- Feels he or she must perform every task perfectly
- Overly impatient with imperfections of others
- Unable to stay on task due to excessive emotion
- Laughing disturbs ability to stay on topic
- Easily distracted, upset by environmental milieu
- Frequent hostile outbursts in groups

EXPRESSION

- Expresses no emotional response
- Superficial emotional response
- Sullen in appearance
- Anger apparent through evasiveness, but denied by patient
- Anger continually expressed in negative physical manner.
- Explosive, unpredictable behavior
- Easily frustrated
- Sulks if means are not met
- Chronic complainer
- Minor events greatly alter mood
- Suspiciousness inhibits group performance
- Verbally responds to internal stimuli
- Preoccupied with carrying out delusional beliefs
- Easily intimidated by peers
- Unable to see positive traits in self
- Patient feels unworthy of anything
- Neglect of physical appearance due to depression
- Excessive crying
- Follows emotional lead of others rather than own feelings
- Unable to recognize emotions of others
- Hypersexual

MANIPULATIVE

- Becomes unnecessarily involved in other's problems
- Gains possessions/favors through intimidation
- Emotional display used as manipulative tool
- Seeks attention through threats/action of self-injurious behavior (SIB)
- Family issues/individual issues hinder treatment process

FLEXIBILITY

- Overly anxious about change
- Overly resistive to change
- Inability to stray from routine
- Needs excessive structure
- Inability to be spontaneous
- Excess observance of rules
- Fearful of leaving treatment center
- Intentionally sabotages discharge plans
- Lack of insight into mental illness
- Unable to see good in any situation

Emotional

TARGET SYMPTOM	LONG-TERM GOAL	SHORT-TERM GOAL	INTERVENTION

Emotional

Group Performance

TARGET SYMPTOM	LONG-TERM GOAL	SHORT-TERM GOAL	INTERVENTION
Uninvolved in therapies.	Patient will be involved in therapies.	Patient will meet with therapist and mutually decide on therapy schedule 1 time by (date).	Therapist to schedule meeting time and provide therapy options to patient.
		Patient will fully participate in 1 group on therapy schedule 3 times weekly.	Therapist to encourage attendance—praise efforts.
Fearful of failing in group situations.	Patient will try new group situations.	Patient will initially try 75% of all required tasks/activities during all scheduled groups.	Therapist will encourage any participation and praise efforts.
		Patient will fully participate in 2 of 3 tasks/activities presented in each group.	Therapist to pair patient with peer to make situation/fear of failure less threatening.
Frustration hinders participation.	Patient participates without becoming frustrated.	Patient will complete assigned tasks in 3 of 5 groups, without verbalizing frustration.	Therapist to offer assistance—encourage as needed.
		Patient will verbalize 2 positive outlets for frustration prior to group 3 times weekly.	Ask patient to verbalize alternative outlets prior to each group.
Feels he or she must perform every task perfectly.	Patient will not criticize self for occasional mistakes.	Patient will state 1 positive thing learned from each mistake made during group task when asked by therapist 100% of time.	Therapist to ask for positives—supply suggestions as needed.
		Patient will attempt to correct all mistakes without bringing it to staff/peers' attention during group tasks 80% of the time.	Therapist to praise patient when mistakes are corrected without bringing to staff/peer attention.

Emotional

TARGET SYMPTOM	LONG-TERM GOAL	SHORT-TERM GOAL	INTERVENTION

Emotional

Group Performance

TARGET SYMPTOM	LONG-TERM GOAL	SHORT-TERM GOAL	INTERVENTION
Overly impatient with imperfections of others.	To be patient with imperfections of others.	Patient will offer assistance in positive manner to peer having difficulty with task in group as directed by therapist 100% of time.	Therapist will direct patient to offer assistance when becoming impatient.
		When asked by therapist, patient will verbalize understanding of differences in abilities 2 of 3 times.	Therapist will allow patient opportunity as needed to discuss differing abilities of others.
Unable to stay on task due to excessive emotion.	Will be able to control emotion enough to stay on task.	Prior to group, patient will identify 2 calming techniques that they can use when feeling overemotional 100% of the time they are asked by therapist.	Therapist to discuss calming techniques with patient as needed.
		When verbalizing frustration in group, patient will demonstrate ability to use calming techniques 50% of time.	Therapist to praise patient when able to successfully calm self.
Laughing disturbs ability to stay on topic.	Patient will be able to stay on group topic/discussion.	Patient will make 1 comment pertinent to discussion topic 1 time every group.	Therapist to redirect patient when laughing—ask for comments on topic.
		Prior to group, patient will be able to verbalize 3 ways to control inappropriate laughter when asked by therapist 100% of time.	Therapist to ask patient to verbalize intervention techniques a minimum of 2 times weekly.

Emotional

TARGET SYMPTOM	LONG-TERM GOAL	SHORT-TERM GOAL	INTERVENTION

Emotional

Group Performance

TARGET SYMPTOM	LONG-TERM GOAL	SHORT-TERM GOAL	INTERVENTION
Easily distracted, upset by environmental milieu.	Patient will remain calm and stay on task regardless of milieu.	Patient will be able to identify distracting aspects of environment and state a minimum of 1 coping strategy 100% of time when asked by therapist.	Therapist to praise/encourage efforts.
		Patient will be able to stay calm and on task in group a minimum of 15 minutes when environment is distracting/stressful 2 of 3 times.	Patient to be reminded of goal—praise all efforts.
Frequent hostile outbursts in groups.	Patient will be able to control own hostility in group.	Patient will remain calm in group a minimum of 50 minutes, per every hour of therapy.	Therapist to confront patient—suggest coping strategies.
		Patient will independently remove self from group when angry and return within 5 minutes in a calm manner 100% of time.	Therapist to remind patient of goal prior to group and praise all independent time outs.

Emotional

TARGET SYMPTOM	LONG-TERM GOAL	SHORT-TERM GOAL	INTERVENTION

Emotional

Expression

TARGET SYMPTOM	LONG-TERM GOAL	SHORT-TERM GOAL	INTERVENTION
Expresses no emotional response.	Patient will be able to express emotions.	Patient will be able to verbally/ nonverbally express 1 sign of emotion in group 80% of groups.	Therapist to provide a nonthreatening environment—encourage any emotional expression.
		Patient will be able to identify 3 emotions they felt in each group session when asked by therapist 3 of 4 times.	Therapist to allow time at end of each session to discuss feelings.
Superficial emotional response.	Patient to express sincere emotional responses.	Patient will report 1 instance of when they did not reveal their *true* emotions and state reasons during each group by (date).	Therapist to ask for examples of displayed superficial emotions.
		Patient will be able to role play a superficial emotional response and identify sincere alternatives 1 time weekly in group.	Therapist to facilitate role play opportunities—encourage participation.
Sullen in appearance.	Patient will show affect when approached.	Patient will participate in role playing of exhibiting different emotional responses to situations 3 times weekly.	Therapist to provide for role play opportunities—encourage interaction.
		Patient will be able to smile and greet each group member at the start of session daily.	Therapist to structure group so patients are required to greet each other.

Emotional

TARGET SYMPTOM	LONG-TERM GOAL	SHORT-TERM GOAL	INTERVENTION

Emotional

Expression

TARGET SYMPTOM	LONG-TERM GOAL	SHORT-TERM GOAL	INTERVENTION
Anger apparent through evasiveness, but denied by patient.	Patient to appropriately express anger when felt.	Patient will be able to identify feelings when confronted by therapist about apparent anger 2 of 3 times.	Therapist to confront patient when anger is apparent.
		Patient will be able to define anger and state one personal reaction to it 80% of time when asked by therapist.	Therapist to ask patient for personal reactions to anger.
Anger continually expressed in negative physical manner.	Anger to be expressed in an appropriate manner.	Patient will be able to state 3 alternatives to physical aggressiveness when angry 100% of the time they are asked by therapist.	Therapist to ask for alternatives and discuss suggestions.
		Patient will demonstrate identified alternative to anger without prompting by therapist 2 of 3 times in group.	Therapist to praise patient when they demonstrate identified alternatives to physical aggression.
Explosive unpredictable behavior.	Patient to express feelings in a calm manner.	When upset, patient will calmly identify source of feeling when requested by therapist 50% of time.	Therapist to ask patient to identify source of anxiety as needed.
		When feeling explosive, patient will leave group for a maximum of 3 minutes and use self-calming techniques before returning in a calm manner 100% of time.	Therapist to excuse patient from group to calm self as needed.

Emotional

TARGET SYMPTOM	LONG-TERM GOAL	SHORT-TERM GOAL	INTERVENTION

Emotional

Expression

TARGET SYMPTOM	LONG-TERM GOAL	SHORT-TERM GOAL	INTERVENTION
Easily frustrated.	Patient will be able to demonstrate tolerance.	When in need of assistance patient will calmly ask for help 2 of 3 times in group.	Therapist to ignore negative demands for help and respond to appropriate request.
		When learning a new task, patient will complete task calmly asking directions as needed 50% of time.	Therapist to give simple step by step directions—praise efforts.
Sulks if means are not met.	Patient to be able to accept disappointments.	Patient will calmly accept decisions made that are contrary to desires 75% of time during group.	Therapist to praise efforts to control sulking behavior.
		Patient will verbalize feeling of disappointment as they occur 80% of time.	Therapist to be available to process feelings—praise appropriate behavior.
Chronic complainer.	Patient will be able to see positives in situation.	Patient will be able to state 1 positive about situation as asked by therapist 3 of 4 times.	When complaining, therapist will ask patient to state positives about situation.
		90% of patient's verbal actions in group will be of a positive nature 3 of 5 days.	Therapist to promote a positive milieu—redirect as necessary.
Minor events greatly alter mood.	Patient to be in a stable mood majority of time.	Patient will be able to cope with everyday occurrences without becoming verbally loud in group 3 of 5 days.	Therapist to confront patient when upset by minor day-to-day events.
		Patient will remain speaking in a calm manner when group milieu becomes distracting 100% of time.	Remind patient of goal as necessary.

Emotional

TARGET SYMPTOM	LONG-TERM GOAL	SHORT-TERM GOAL	INTERVENTION

Emotional

Expression

TARGET SYMPTOM	LONG-TERM GOAL	SHORT-TERM GOAL	INTERVENTION
Suspiciousness inhibits group performance.	Patient to function in group despite suspiciousness.	Patient will be able to identify one feeling of suspiciousness and discuss faulty reasoning 1 time weekly when requested by therapist.	Therapist to discuss suspicious feelings with patient a minimum of 1 time weekly.
		Despite suspicious feelings, patient will fully participate in group 75% of time 3 times weekly.	Therapist to give reassurance/ support when patient has identified feelings of suspiciousness.
Verbally responds to internal stimuli.	Patient will be focused in group regardless of internal stimuli.	Patient will identify 1 time when he or she was being directed by external stimuli by (date).	Therapist to help patient identify feelings—encourage discussion.
		Patient will be able to identify/ suggest 3 coping mechanisms to deal with stimuli when asked by therapist 50% of time.	Therapist to ask patient for ways to cope with internal stimuli 1 time every group.
Preoccupied with carrying out delusional beliefs.	Patient will be able to identify belief as delusional, and control actions of carrying out.	Patient will discuss delusional belief with therapist and point out faulty logic when asked by therapist 100% of time.	Therapist will discuss patient's delusions/faulty logic a minimum of 1 time weekly.
		Patient will identify 1 coping technique to be used when delusions are present as requested by therapist 80% of time.	Therapist will ask patient to identify personal coping technique a minimum of 1 time weekly.

Emotional

TARGET SYMPTOM	LONG-TERM GOAL	SHORT-TERM GOAL	INTERVENTION

Emotional

Expression

TARGET SYMPTOM	LONG-TERM GOAL	SHORT-TERM GOAL	INTERVENTION
Easily intimidated by peers.	Patient will be assertive with peers.	Patient will be able to identify 1 situation in which he or she feels intimidated a minimum of 1 time weekly in group.	Therapist to allow time in group to discuss issues of intimidation a minimum of 1 time weekly.
		Patient will be able to say "no" to peers asking for goods 75% of time as observed by therapist.	Therapist to involve patient in role playing assertiveness a minimum of 2 times monthly in group.
Unable to see positive traits in self.	Patient will be able to point out positives in self.	Patient will be able to identify 2 positive traits in self when asked by therapist 75% of time.	Therapist will ask patient to identify positives in self a minimum of 2 times weekly.
		Patient will identify 2 past accomplishments and 2 future goals to entire group when asked by therapist 75% of time.	Therapist to ask group to share accomplishments/goals minimum of 1 time weekly.
Patient feels unworthy of anything.	Patient to express feelings of self-worth.	Patient will be able to identify feelings of unworthiness 1 time weekly when asked by therapist.	Therapist to ask patient to identify and discuss feelings of unworthiness a minimum of 3 times weekly.
		Patient to be able to accept compliments/gifts with a verbal "thank you" a minimum of 1 time weekly without disclaiming worth.	Therapist to compliment/offer tokens to patient a minimum of 3 times weekly.
Neglect of physical appearance due to depression.	Patient will maintain hygiene/personal appearance.	Patient will be able to identify 2 positive effects of good grooming 75% of time when asked by therapist.	Therapist to ask patient to identify the positives of being well-groomed a minimum of 2 times weekly.
		Patient will be neat and clean in appearance 2 of 3 days weekly.	Therapist to encourage patient to work on grooming—praise efforts.

Emotional

TARGET SYMPTOM	LONG-TERM GOAL	SHORT-TERM GOAL	INTERVENTION

Emotional

Expression

TARGET SYMPTOM	LONG-TERM GOAL	SHORT-TERM GOAL	INTERVENTION
Excessive crying.	Patient to decrease amount of time spent crying.	Patient will be able to identify reason for crying 90% of time when asked by therapist.	Therapist to ask patient reason for crying—encourage response.
		Patient will stop crying when asked by therapist 50% of time.	Therapist will ask patient to cease crying—praise successful attempts.
Follows emotional lead of others rather than own feelings.	Patient to react emotionally primarily to own feelings.	When subjected to others' emotional outbursts which do not affect him or her, patient will remain involved in group 100% of time.	Therapist to praise patient when he or she exhibits control of feelings.
		Patient when confronted by therapist will be able to state reason for change in emotion 3 of 4 times.	Therapist to confront patient when labile and process feelings.
Unable to recognize emotions in others.	Patient will be able to recognize and differentiate feelings of others.	Patient will be able to correctly identify emotions of others 80% of time in role play situations.	Therapist will give patient opportunity to be involved in role playing and identifying emotions and groups.
		For each situation presented by therapist in group, patient will be able to identify 2 common, appropriate emotional responses 3 of 5 times.	Therapist to state hypothetical situations and ask for possible/probable emotional reactions.
Hypersexual	Patient will be sexually appropriate.	Patient will interact in group settings without sexually harassing comments 95% of time.	Therapist to remove patient from group if harassment continues after 1 warning.
		Patient will be able to identify own hypersexual remarks/actions 80% of time when asked by therapist.	Therapist will ask patient to identify his or her hypersexual action and discuss alternative outlets.

Emotional

TARGET SYMPTOM	LONG-TERM GOAL	SHORT-TERM GOAL	INTERVENTION

Emotional

Manipulative

TARGET SYMPTOM	LONG-TERM GOAL	SHORT-TERM GOAL	INTERVENTION
Becomes unnecessarily involved in others' problems.	Patient will have minimal involvement in others' problems.	Patient will limit discussions of peers' problems to a maximum of 5 minutes in 100% of groups.	Therapist to confront patient when becoming overly involved in others—direct to deal only with own problems.
		Patient will be able to decline invitation to help peers with their problems 2 of 3 requests per group.	Therapist to help patient be assertive with peers when assistance is required.
Gains possessions/favors through intimidation.	Patient will gain goods without intimidating others.	When asking for goods, patient will accept "no" for an answer 75% of time without further pressuring peer as observed by therapist.	Therapist to provide opportunities to role play aggressive/assertive behavior.
		When asked by therapist, patient will be able to identify own intimidating behaviors and give one nonintimidating alternative behavior 3 of 4 times.	Confront—redirect when patient intimidates peers.
Emotional display used as a manipulative tool.	Patient will be sincere in exhibited emotions.	Patient will be able to identify 1 personal manipulative behavior 1 time per group.	Therapist to ask patient to identify manipulative behaviors.
		Patient will role play appropriate emotional response in group a minimum of 2 times monthly.	Therapist to provide opportunity for role play—encourage participation.

Emotional

47

TARGET SYMPTOM	LONG-TERM GOAL	SHORT-TERM GOAL	INTERVENTION

Emotional

Manipulative

TARGET SYMPTOM	LONG-TERM GOAL	SHORT-TERM GOAL	INTERVENTION
Seeks attention through action/ threats of self-injurious behavior (SIB).	Patient to seek attention through positive means.	When in need of personal attention, patient will verbally request it 4 of 5 times.	Therapist to praise patient when he or she asks for attention in positive way.
		Patient will be able to state 2 negatives of self-injurious behavior threats when asked by therapist 80% of time.	Therapist will ask patient to point out negatives of threatening self-injurious behavior 1 time weekly per group.
Family issues/individual issues hinder treatment progress.	Patient to progress with treatment despite family/individual issues.	Patient will actively participate in planned treatment 80% of group time.	Therapist to encourage active involvement in treatment—praise efforts.
		Patient to state 2 advantages of working through treatment when asked by therapist 75% of time.	Therapist to encourage patient to verbalize advantages of working through treatment.

Emotional

TARGET SYMPTOM	LONG-TERM GOAL	SHORT-TERM GOAL	INTERVENTION

Emotional

Flexibility

TARGET SYMPTOM	LONG-TERM GOAL	SHORT-TERM GOAL	INTERVENTION
Overly anxious about change.	Patient to express satisfaction with current/upcoming changes.	Patient to verbalize what makes him or her uncomfortable about a changing situation when asked by therapist 80% of time.	Therapist to encourage patient to talk about what makes them anxious with regard to change.
		When asked by therapist, patient will state 2 coping mechanisms which calm him or her when anxious about change 100% of time.	Therapist to encourage patient to utilize personal coping mechanisms—quiz patient periodically on use.
Overly resistive to change.	Patient will be receptive to change.	When in group, patient will discuss pros/cons of change before making a decision about change 75% of time.	Therapist will help patient weigh pros/cons of situation—encourage compliance.
		When asked by therapist, patient will break down anxiety producing change into small manageable steps 3 of 4 times.	Therapist will ask patient to break down change when expressing anxiety.
Inability to stray from routine.	Patient amenable to changes in routine.	Patient will discuss 1 way to vary from routine 2 times weekly in group.	Therapist to ask patient a minimum of 2 times weekly for variations to routine—provide suggestions as needed.
		Patient will discuss 1 advantage of varying daily routine when asked by therapist 1 time weekly.	Therapist to encourage flexibility—praise efforts.

Emotional

TARGET SYMPTOM	LONG-TERM GOAL	SHORT-TERM GOAL	INTERVENTION

Emotional

Flexibility

TARGET SYMPTOM	LONG-TERM GOAL	SHORT-TERM GOAL	INTERVENTION
Needs excessive structure.	Patient to function independently with minimal structure.	When given instructions patient will be able to finish task in group without asking for additional instructions/help 25% of the time.	Therapist to give simple, easy to follow directions—clarify expectations.
		Patient will engage in 1 leisure activity with peer in an unstructured environment 1 time weekly as reported by patient.	Therapist to provide leisure activity chart for patient to keep account of progress toward goal.
Inability to be spontaneous.	Patient to be able to show spontaneity.	Patient will be able to give 1 example of spontaneous behavior when given role play situations 1 time weekly.	Therapist to provide role play situations weekly.
		Patient when asked by therapist to attend an off-grounds activity, will agree without any further deliberation 2 times monthly.	Therapist to ask patient to attend off-grounds activities on a regular basis.
Excess observance of rules.	Observance of rules is moderated by circumstances.	Patient will be able to state 1 situation in which circumstances mandate a rule change during group discussion a minimum of 1 time weekly.	Therapist to provide opportunities for discussion.
		Patient will be able to identify 1 example when rules need to be changed in order to successfully accomplish a group task 1 time weekly.	Patient to be assigned leadership role and given authority to change rules as needed.

Emotional

TARGET SYMPTOM	LONG-TERM GOAL	SHORT-TERM GOAL	INTERVENTION

Emotional

Flexibility

TARGET SYMPTOM	LONG-TERM GOAL	SHORT-TERM GOAL	INTERVENTION
Fearful of leaving treatment center.	Patient to be comfortable leaving treatment center.	Patient will attend off-grounds outings a minimum of 2 times monthly.	Therapist to personally invite patient to off-grounds outings.
		Patient will go on pass into community a minimum of 2 times monthly.	Therapist to encourage passes—assist in planning as needed.
Intentionally sabotages discharge plans.	Patient will cooperate with discharge planning.	Upon request, patient will state 3 negative consequences of sabotaging discharge plans to peers during group 75% of time.	Therapist to ask for consequences daily in group, and provide opportunities for discussion—confront as necessary.
		Patient will complete 3 tasks related to pursuing discharge by (date).	Therapist to regularly suggest positive action steps for discharge—encourage and ask for progress.
Lack of insight into mental illness.	Patient will express insight into mental illness.	Patient will verbally acknowledge 1 symptom of his or her mental illness during group discussion 1 time weekly.	Therapist to ask patient for symptoms, provide time for discussion, praise efforts—confront as needed.
		Patient will be able to state 3 ways mental illness has affected his or her life, when asked by therapist 75% of time during group.	Therapist will discuss effects of mental illness daily in group—encourage personal insights.
Unable to see good in any situation.	Patient will see both positives and negatives in all situations.	With direction, patient will be able to state 1 positive in a role play situation 1 time weekly in group.	Therapist to involve patient in role plays weekly—encourage all positive remarks.
		Patient able to state 2 positive outcomes from an initially negative situation when requested by therapist 2 of 3 times during group discussion.	Therapist to ask patient for sample situations—encourage patient to look for positives.

Emotional

55

- Language barrier
- Unable to comply with verbal directions
- Difficulty expressing self due to lack of verbal/writing skills
- Needs continual prompting cues in group
- Slow to respond
- Unable to make decisions for self
- Concrete in thinking
- Preoccupied
- Easily distracted, short attention span
- Difficulty learning rules
- No functional reading ability
- Poor short-term memory
- Poor long-term memory
- Minimal purposeful interaction with environment
- Unable to discriminate colors
- Poor judge of safety
- Low IQ, difficulty keeping up with peers
- Difficulty following conversation

Intellectual

TARGET SYMPTOM	LONG-TERM GOAL	SHORT-TERM GOAL	INTERVENTION

Intellectual

TARGET SYMPTOM	LONG-TERM GOAL	SHORT-TERM GOAL	INTERVENTION
Language barrier.	To communicate effectively despite barrier.	Patient will be able to ask for needed materials in group 1 time through nonverbal communication 2 of 3 groups.	Therapist will encourage patient to make needs known—praise all attempts at communication.
		Patient will convey 1 comment to peer 1 time every group using both verbal and nonverbal communication.	Therapist to facilitate peer interactions.
Unable to comply with verbal directions.	Patient to follow verbal directions.	Patient will follow 50% of all verbal directions given in group by therapist.	Therapist will, along with verbal directions, use gestures and body language to convey messages.
		Patient will independently follow 1 verbal direction given by therapist 1 time daily in group.	Therapist to give clear concise directions—clarify expectations.
Difficulty expressing self due to lack of verbal skills.	Patient to express feelings through facial expression feelings chart.	Patient will respond to feeling questions by pointing out to feelings chart which correctly identifies his or her emotion.	Therapist to instruct patient on use of chart—encourage use.
		Patient will show feelings/convey messages through facial expression 75% of the time when asked for feedback from therapist.	Therapist to work with patient on how to correctly convey commonly understood gestures and facial expressions.
Needs continual prompting, cues in group.	Patient will complete tasks, respond to questions without continual prompting.	Patient will follow 75% of directions given a minimum of 3 cues/prompts in group 2 of 3 days.	Therapist to give clear, easy to follow directions after gaining attention of patient.
		Patient will be able to complete 2 tasks each group period without any prompts or reminders.	Therapist to praise patient for successfully completing each task without additional help/cues.

Intellectual

59

TARGET SYMPTOM	LONG-TERM GOAL	SHORT-TERM GOAL	INTERVENTION

Intellectual

TARGET SYMPTOM	LONG-TERM GOAL	SHORT-TERM GOAL	INTERVENTION
Slow to respond.	Patient to respond to questions without hesitation.	Patient will respond to 50% of all questions asked during group with no more than a 5 second delay.	Therapist to repeat questions to patient if no response is given after 5 seconds.
		Patient will immediately respond to all questions/comments when in social situation with peers 100% of time as observed by therapist.	Therapist to praise patient as progress is made.
Unable to make decisions for self.	Patient to make decisions for self.	Patient, when given a choice, will make a decision by themselves 50% of time.	Therapist to offer 2 choices to patient and encourage patient to make a decision.
		Patient will make 50% of group decisions, without consulting others for opinions, when asked by therapist.	Therapist to encourage independent decision making—praise efforts.
Concrete in thinking.	Patient to look at different options before making decisions.	When given role play situations, patient will state 2 alternative options 100% of time.	Therapist will provide role play opportunities weekly.
		Patient to look at different options before making any decisions.	Therapist to provide problem-solving opportunities in structured group.

TARGET SYMPTOM	LONG-TERM GOAL	SHORT-TERM GOAL	INTERVENTION

Intellectual

TARGET SYMPTOM	LONG-TERM GOAL	SHORT-TERM GOAL	INTERVENTION
Preoccupied.	Patient to be attentive to environment.	Patient will answer 75% of questions asked of them without more than a 5 second delay while in groups.	Therapist to encourage patient to be attentive and stay on task.
		Patient will be able to repeat directions given 50% of time when asked by therapist.	Therapist will ask patient to repeat directions a minimum of 1 time per group setting.
Easily distracted, short attention span.	Patient will stay on tasks.	Patient will maintain eye contact with group members/milieu as observed by therapist 50% of time.	Therapist to provide structure—praise all efforts.
		Patient will stay on task in group a minimum of 10 minutes daily in 2 of 3 groups weekly.	Therapist will redirect patient as necessary—praise efforts.
Difficulty learning rules.	Patient to comprehend set rules.	Patient will be able to repeat 3 game rules to therapist when asked 50% of time.	Therapist to ask patient to repeat rules as necessary.
		Patient will explain rules of one game in group correctly as observed by therapist.	Therapist to ask patient to explain rules to group after patient has been taught game.

Intellectual

TARGET SYMPTOM	LONG-TERM GOAL	SHORT-TERM GOAL	INTERVENTION

Intellectual

TARGET SYMPTOM	LONG-TERM GOAL	SHORT-TERM GOAL	INTERVENTION
No functional reading ability.	Function in group despite lack of reading ability.	Patient will partner with peer and cooperatively work together in activities where some reading is required 100% of time in group.	Therapist will pair partner with compatible peer, praise cooperative efforts.
		Patient to express self verbally rather than on paper 100% of time in groups where worksheets are presented.	Therapist to inform patient that verbal responses rather than written are acceptable, encourage responses.
Poor short-term memory.	Patient will compensate for memory loss.	Patient will be able to state 1 of 4 upcoming events 1 hour after being told by therapist 3 of 5 days per week.	Therapist to review events daily, ask for recall 1 hour later.
		Patient will state 3 ways he or she can compensate for poor memory when asked by therapist 75% of time.	Therapist to educate patient on ways to compensate for memory impairment, review daily.
Poor long-term memory.	Patient will compensate for memory loss.	Patient to identify 1 positive memory about leisure experience 1 time weekly in reminiscing group.	Therapist to facilitate discussion, cueing patient with a variety of sensory materials (e.g., photos, music).
		Patient to write in journal 1 time daily including information on personal experiences and interests as observed by therapist.	Therapist to encourage journal writing to use as a memory tool.

Intellectual

TARGET SYMPTOM	LONG-TERM GOAL	SHORT-TERM GOAL	INTERVENTION

Intellectual

TARGET SYMPTOM	LONG-TERM GOAL	SHORT-TERM GOAL	INTERVENTION
Minimal purposeful interaction with environment.	Interacts purposefully with people/objects.	Patient to show awareness of object in environment by pointing out object verbally stated by therapist 1 time per 1-to-1 session.	Therapist to practice object recognition in 1-to-1 sessions by pointing to object and reciting word.
		When asked by therapist, patient will make eye contact and maintain for a minimum of 5 seconds 1 of 4 times during 1-to-1 session.	Therapist to encourage eye contact during 1-to-1 session.
Unable to discriminate colors.	Patient to compensate for color blindness.	Patient will state colors he or she cannot correctly identify 100% of time when asked by therapist.	Therapist to test ability to distinguish colors—review results with patient.
		Patient will discuss a minimum of 2 ways to adapt a table game involving "problem" colors with therapist prior to playing game 100% of time in group.	Therapist to offer suggestions for game adaptations.
Poor judge of safety.	Patient to adhere to safety rules and regulations.	Patient will identify proper procedure for emergency drill 100% of time when asked by therapist.	Therapist to familiarize patient with safety procedures.
		Patient will be able to identify 3 potentially dangerous situations and the appropriate actions to take 1 time per discussion per topic.	Therapist to provide role play situations—encourage problem solving.

Intellectual

TARGET SYMPTOM	LONG-TERM GOAL	SHORT-TERM GOAL	INTERVENTION

Intellectual

TARGET SYMPTOM	LONG-TERM GOAL	SHORT-TERM GOAL	INTERVENTION
Low IQ, difficulty keeping up with peers.	Will be able to participate equally with peers despite low IQ.	Patient will be able to identify areas in which they are having trouble within 10 minutes after start of activity when asked by therapist 75% of time.	Therapist to ask patient to identify problem areas—assist as needed.
		Patient will identify a minimum of 2 activities they feel competent engaging in with peers in group by (date).	Therapist to expose patient to a variety of leisure activities.
Difficulty following conversation.	Will be able to follow conversation.	After 5 minutes of group discussion, patient will be able to relate 2 facts regarding discussion when asked by therapist 50% of time.	Therapist to facilitate group discussion—ask patient to recite specifics.
		Patient will identify 2 "memory cues" to aid them in following a conversation when asked by therapist 1 time weekly in group.	Therapist to identify memory cue techniques, e.g., eye contact, word association, repeating information.

Intellectual

- Poor balance
- Poor coordination
- Impaired mobility
- Underweight
- Obesity
- Lethargic
- Avoids physical activity
- Difficulty hearing
- Unable to pronounce words clearly
- Poor vision
- Refuses to follow diabetic diet
- Water intoxication
- Incontinent
- Side effects—acathisia
- Poor hand-eye coordination
- Low endurance, tires easily
- Capable, but unwilling to propel own wheelchair
- Bedridden
- Poor large motor coordination
- Seizures

Physical

TARGET SYMPTOM	LONG-TERM GOAL	SHORT-TERM GOAL	INTERVENTION

P h y s i c a l

TARGET SYMPTOM	LONG-TERM GOAL	SHORT-TERM GOAL	INTERVENTION
Poor balance.	Adjust for poor balance.	When in gym group, patient will walk through games rather than run 100% of the time.	Therapist will modify games to fit patient's needs.
		Patient will be able to identify 2 ways to cope with poor balance when asked by therapist by (date).	Therapist to assist patient in problem solving—offer suggestions as needed.
Poor coordination.	Increase coordination/safely participate.	Patient will be able to state 1 safety issue relating to poor coordination prior to participating in gym group each day.	Therapist will encourage patient to work on hand-eye coordination exercises/activities a minimum of 15 minutes daily.
		Patient will ask therapist to recommend exercises to improve coordination 1 time by (date).	Therapist to be available to assist patient when needed.
Impaired mobility.	Ambulate with minimal assistance.	Patient will walk to group independently with assistive device 2 of 3 times weekly.	Therapist will encourage group attendance—praise successful attempts of arriving at group.
		Patient will provide 2 suggestions that will assist in maneuvering if unable to attend group unaided, when asked by therapist.	Therapist will encourage problem-solving behavior when asked to help in maneuvering.
Underweight.	Maintain ideal weight.	Patient, when in gym group, will follow exercise regimen set by therapist 80% of time.	Therapist will encourage compliance of set exercise regimen, discourage compulsive excessive activity.
		Patient will be able to state 2 positive reasons for maintaining ideal body weight when asked by therapist by (date).	Therapist will point out positives in maintaining ideal body weight, allow opportunity for discussion.

Physical

TARGET SYMPTOM	LONG-TERM GOAL	SHORT-TERM GOAL	INTERVENTION

Physical

TARGET SYMPTOM	LONG-TERM GOAL	SHORT-TERM GOAL	INTERVENTION
Obesity.	Maintain ideal weight.	Patient will engage in 30 minutes of physical activity 4 of 5 days weekly in gym group.	Therapist will encourage physical activity—provide exercise outlets through gym/swim groups.
		Patient will be able to identify and carry out 2 active leisure alternatives to eating each weekend by (date).	Therapist to provide leisure education—encourage nonsedentary activities.
Lethargic.	Increased enthusiasm/motivation.	Patient will be on time to 75% of assigned therapy groups—without prompts from therapist.	Therapist will assign groups and praise good attendance.
		Patient will be able to identify 2 means of increasing energy level during daytime hours 2 of 3 times when asked by therapist.	Therapist to provide opportunity for patient to discuss and problem-solve issues of decreased energy.
Avoids physical activity.	Engage in physical activities.	Patient will actively participate in 2 active leisure groups weekly.	Therapist to provide active leisure groups—encourage participation.
		Patient will be able to identify 4 positive outcomes from regularly engaging in physical activity when asked by therapist by (date).	Therapist to regularly discuss benefits of physical exercise and engage patients in discussions.
Difficulty hearing.	Increase listening skills.	Patient will be able to repeat back to therapist instructions given when asked—a minimum of 1 time weekly.	Therapist will encourage patient to ask for directions to be repeated when unable to hear original instructions being given.
		Patient will situate self by therapist in groups so as to better hear instructions 100% of time.	Therapist to encourage/praise compliance.

Physical

TARGET SYMPTOM	LONG-TERM GOAL	SHORT-TERM GOAL	INTERVENTION

Physical

TARGET SYMPTOM	LONG-TERM GOAL	SHORT-TERM GOAL	INTERVENTION
Unable to pronounce words clearly.	Communicate with increased effectiveness.	Patient will speak to peers only after they have made eye contact when in group 75% of time.	Therapist to encourage patient to gain eye contact before speaking to others.
		Patient will repeat statements as necessary when others ask for clarification of conversation 100% of time.	Therapist will encourage goal compliance, praise patient when patience has been demonstrated without frustration interfering.
Poor vision.	Compensate for poor vision.	When having difficulty due to poor vision, patient will ask for assistance with projects they are unable to complete 2 times by (date).	Therapist to encourage patient to ask for needed assistance.
		When asked by therapist, patient will be able to identify 2 ways to compensate when vision hinders participation 100% of time.	Therapist to encourage patient to problem solve and identify techniques for overcoming barriers.
Refuses to follow diabetic diet.	Patient to follow diabetic diet.	Patient, when in groups and activities where food is served, will follow diabetic diet 100% of time.	Therapist will praise efforts— remind patient as necessary.
		Patient will be able to state 1 reason to follow diabetic diet when asked by therapist in group by (date).	Therapist to discuss diabetic diet with patient and point out its importance.

Physical

TARGET SYMPTOM	LONG-TERM GOAL	SHORT-TERM GOAL	INTERVENTION

Physical

TARGET SYMPTOM	LONG-TERM GOAL	SHORT-TERM GOAL	INTERVENTION
Water intoxication.	Patient will adhere to liquid limitations.	When on off-grounds outings, patient will not consume liquids which exceed set limit 100% of the time.	Therapist to inform patient of liquid limits—encourage compliance.
		Patient will be able to state 2 negative reactions from drinking excess liquids when asked by therapist 2 of 3 times.	Therapist to discuss problems associated with water intoxication—encourage compliance.
Incontinent.	Function despite incontinence.	Patient will independently prepare themselves for possible incontinence during outing 100% of the time as judged by therapist.	Therapist to inform patient of goal—encourage compliance.
		Patient to identify a minimum of 2 ways to cope with possible incontinence 1 time weekly prior to activity.	Therapist to ask patient to identify coping mechanisms for incontinence prior to all outings.
Side effects—acathisia.	Function in groups despite side effects.	Prior to group, patient will identify 2 ways to cope with acathisia, (i.e., walking around) that will enable them to remain in group room for the entire session 2 of 3 times per week.	Therapist to ask patient for coping mechanisms prior to group.
		Patient will be able to identify a minimum of 1 activity they could engage in while feeling side effects of acathisia when asked by therapist.	Therapist to encourage patient to explore different activities—discuss options.

Physical

TARGET SYMPTOM	LONG-TERM GOAL	SHORT-TERM GOAL	INTERVENTION

Physical

TARGET SYMPTOM	LONG-TERM GOAL	SHORT-TERM GOAL	INTERVENTION
Poor hand-eye coordination.	Adapt tasks as necessary for poor hand-eye coordination.	Patient to identify need for activity adaptations when poor hand-eye coordination prohibits participation in group 100% of time as judged by therapist.	Therapist to encourage patient to be aware of limitations and express difficulties.
		Patient will participate in a minimum of 3 new adapted games per month per group.	Therapist to provide and encourage use of adaptive devices.
Low endurance, tires easily.	Increase endurance.	Patient to increase walking distance from 1/4 mile to 1/2 mile after 4 weeks of regular exercise.	Therapist to introduce exercise to increase patient's endurance and stamina.
		Patient to participate in physically active team sports a minimum of 30 minutes per 1 hour group in gym 3 of 5 days weekly.	Therapist to encourage participation—praise all efforts.
Capable, but unwilling to propel own wheelchair.	Propel own wheelchair.	Patient will propel self to 1 group daily without assistance from staff for 5 consecutive days by (date).	Therapist to offer tangibles to patient for successful attempts to attend group unaided.
		Patient to engage in strengthening exercises 3 times weekly to build endurance to propel self in wheelchair.	Therapist to develop exercise plan to aid in strengthening muscles and increasing stamina.

Physical

TARGET SYMPTOM	LONG-TERM GOAL	SHORT-TERM GOAL	INTERVENTION

Physical

TARGET SYMPTOM	LONG-TERM GOAL	SHORT-TERM GOAL	INTERVENTION
Bedridden.	Involved in daily activities despite physical condition.	Patient to work a minimum of 1/2 hour daily on chosen craft/activity 3 of 5 days as observed by therapist.	Therapist to assess patient's leisure interests—provide opportunities to participate.
		Patient to engage socially with peer(s) 1 time daily for a minimum of 10 minutes 4 of 5 days as observed by therapist.	Therapist to introduce peers—facilitate interaction.
Poor large motor coordination.	Able to participate despite limitations.	Patient will comply with therapist's directions to adapt activity 100% with no more than 1 reminder by (date).	Therapist to adapt activities to ensure patient safety—encourage compliance.
		Patient to identify 2 ways to cope with poor coordination when in large gatherings during problem-solving activities in group 50% of time.	Therapist to help patient identify potential problems and coping mechanisms.
Seizures.	Safely participate despite seizures.	When in swim group, patient will independently put on a personal flotation device and remain in designated area of pool without reminders 100% of time.	Therapist to assist patient in identifying precautionary measures—encourage follow through.
		Patient to identify and follow through with one precautionary measure (i.e., wearing helmet) prior to every community outing as observed by therapist.	Therapist to assist patient in identifying precautionary measures—encourage follow through.

Physical

- Unaware of importance of leisure
- Unaware of leisure resources
- Lacks motivation for leisure involvement
- Difficulty setting aside time for leisure
- Leisure hindered by physical problems
- Limited leisure skills
- Lacks companionship in leisure
- Limited money available for leisure
- Leisure barrier—lack of transportation
- Use of alcohol a barrier to leisure involvement

Leisure

TARGET SYMPTOM	LONG-TERM GOAL	SHORT-TERM GOAL	INTERVENTION

Leisure

TARGET SYMPTOM	LONG-TERM GOAL	SHORT-TERM GOAL	INTERVENTION
Unaware of importance of leisure.	Patient will be knowledgeable about the importance of leisure.	Patient will be able to identify 2 positive outcomes from 1 leisure involvement in the past week during group 1 time weekly.	Therapist will ask for positive outcomes weekly.
		During a role play situation in group, patient will be able to identify positives derived from leisure involvement 1 time weekly.	Discussion of leisure involvement and role play situations done weekly in group.
Unaware of leisure resources.	Patient to be aware of leisure resources.	Patient will be able to identify a minimum of 10 leisure resources available to public when asked by therapist 75% of time.	Therapist to educate patient about the availability of leisure resources in the community.
		Patient will be able to locate resources through use of newspaper as asked by therapist 1 time weekly 100% of time.	Therapist to teach patient how and where to look up community events and recreational opportunity in the daily newspaper.
Lacks motivation for leisure involvement.	Patient to be motivated to engage in leisure activities.	Patient will be able to identify 5 reasons why leisure is important in a person's day-to-day living by (date).	Therapist to discuss the importance of leisure in one's life during leisure groups.
		Patient will follow through with contract of engaging in 1 leisure activity 1 time per weekend for 4 consecutive weeks.	Therapist to have group members contract to engage in 1 leisure activity 1 time per week.

Leisure

TARGET SYMPTOM	LONG-TERM GOAL	SHORT-TERM GOAL	INTERVENTION

L e i s u r e

TARGET SYMPTOM	LONG-TERM GOAL	SHORT-TERM GOAL	INTERVENTION
Difficulty setting aside time for leisure.	Patient will set aside time weekly for leisure.	Patient will demonstrate ability to block out a minimum of 4 hours for leisure pursuit each week.	Therapist will stress the importance of leisure and assist patient in scheduling as necessary.
		Patient will identify 1 leisure activity that they will engage in during that week each Monday session 100% of time.	Therapist will allow time each Monday for patients to plan leisure schedule.
Leisure hindered by physical problems.	Patient to be fulfilled in their leisure despite their physical limitation.	When asked by therapist, patient will be able to identify 5 leisure activities that they enjoy and can engage in despite their limitations by (date).	Therapist to introduce a wide variety of leisure options and encourage patient to explore the possibilities of engaging with their limitations in mind.
		Patients will be able to identify 1 activity that they can do for every activity that poses a barrier, 4 of 5 times asked.	Therapist will present activities to patients that pose as a barrier and request that, in return, they identify ones in which they are capable of engaging.
Limited leisure skills.	Patient will demonstrate skill in leisure activities.	Patient will be knowledgeable in the rules of 3 board games of choice, explaining game rules correctly a minimum of 1 time weekly.	Therapist to teach patient games of his or her choice and ask for rule identification a minimum of 1 time weekly.
		Patient will be able to demonstrate 1 new leisure skill he or she has learned by (date).	Therapist will teach patient a variety of new activities and encourage practice and participation on own.

L e i s u r e

TARGET SYMPTOM	LONG-TERM GOAL	SHORT-TERM GOAL	INTERVENTION

Leisure

TARGET SYMPTOM	LONG-TERM GOAL	SHORT-TERM GOAL	INTERVENTION
Lacks companionship in leisure.	Patient will identify activities that can be done alone, or that do not require personal acquaintance.	Patient will identify 1 leisure resource where he or she can go and be with people in leisure without knowing them personally, when asked by therapist 1 time weekly.	Therapist will teach means to get acquainted with others, e.g., health clubs, dance lessons, associations.
		Patient will identify 1 activity that he or she enjoys that does not require a second person to engage in it 1 time per group.	Therapist to encourage patients to engage in activities that can be done in one's own free time.
Limited money available for leisure.	Patient will be able to identify leisure activities which are free of charge.	When asked by therapist, patient will be able to state 3 activities he or she could do that day which are free of charge 2 of 3 times.	Therapist will help patients identify activities that do not require money during leisure education sessions.
		Patient will be able to plan an entire Saturday, engaging in only activities that are free of charge by (date).	Therapist to encourage leisure planning and assign task of planning a "Free Saturday."
Leisure barrier—lack of transportation.	Patient will engage in leisure activities despite barrier.	Patient will be able to identify 3 leisure activities available to him or her that do not require transportation when asked by therapist 1 time weekly.	Therapist will educate patient on the local events and activities that require no transportation.
		Patient will be able to identify 2 possible transportation alternatives available to him or her for every activity presented by therapist 50% of time.	Therapist will ask patient to problem solve ways to get to activities offered where transportation is needed.

Leisure

TARGET SYMPTOM	LONG-TERM GOAL	SHORT-TERM GOAL	INTERVENTION

Leisure

TARGET SYMPTOM	LONG-TERM GOAL	SHORT-TERM GOAL	INTERVENTION
Use of alcohol a barrier to leisure involvement.	Patient to pursue leisure interests despite barrier.	Patient will identify 3 activities that they can substitute for drinking when feeling the need for alcohol when asked by therapist 100% of time.	Therapist to encourage patients to refrain from activities that in the past were personally associated to alcohol consumption.
		Patient will be able to identify 2 positive outcomes from 1 leisure involvement in the past week during group 1 time weekly.	Therapist to encourage patients to substitute healthy leisure alternatives to drinking.

Leisure

—OTHER BOOKS FROM VENTURE PUBLISHING—

Venture Publishing, Inc.
1999 Cato Avenue
State College, PA 16801
Phone (814) 234-4561
FAX (814) 234-1651

TARGET SYMPTOM	LONG-TERM GOAL	SHORT-TERM GOAL	INTERVENTION

TARGET SYMPTOM	LONG-TERM GOAL	SHORT-TERM GOAL	INTERVENTION